Latter-day Saint Missionaries in the 1976 Guatemala Earthquake

By
Larry Richman

CENTURY PUBLISHING
SALT LAKE CITY, UTAH
FEBRUARY 2026

Latter-day Saint Missionaries in the 1976 Guatemala Earthquake

February 2026

Printed edition, ISBN 978-0-941846-32-5

Copyright © 2026 by Century Publishing, LLC

All rights reserved. No part of this book may be reproduced in any form or by any means without permission in writing from the publisher, Century Publishing, LLC, 7533 S Center View CT Ste R, West Jordan, UT 84084

centurypubl.com

info@centurypubl.com

Printed in the United States of America.

Table of Contents

Table of Contents 1
Introduction 2
The Earthquake 3
   Missionaries in Comalapa 4
   Members in Comalapa 9
   Gathering and Organizing our Forces 12
   Heading Out of Comalapa 13
   Patzicía Church 14
   Missionaries in Patzicía 22
      Senior Agricultural Missionary Couple 22
      Elders in the Language Class 25
      Language Teachers 31
   Missionaries in Sumpango 32
   Missionaries in Patzún 33
   22 Members Killed—15 in Patzicía 34
   Continuing to Patzún 40
   Returning to Patzicía 42
   Returning to Comalapa 45
   Concern From Parents 47
   Relief came quickly 51
Work Camp Patzicía 54
   The Conclusion of Camp Patzicía 122
Pablo Choc 130
Daniel Choc 143

INTRODUCTION

Special 50th Anniversary Edition

This book commemorates the 50th anniversary of the earthquake in 1976 by relating the experiences of some of the missionaries of The Church of Jesus Christ of Latter-day Saints who were serving in Guatemala at that time.

It also includes a special tribute to Pablo Choc, Patzicía branch president, and his son Daniel Choc, who was the first missionary from Patzicía and the Church's first Cakchiquel missionary.

At 3:03:33am on February 4, 1976, an earthquake hit Guatemala. 23,000-25,000 people died, 80,000 were injured, 250,000 homes were destroyed, and nearly 1.5 million inhabitants were left without shelter.

Read a summary of the devastation caused by the Guatemalan earthquake of 1976.

More details about the missionaries mentioned in this book can be found at LarryRichman.org/mission.

This work is not a publication of The Church of Jesus Christ of Latter-day Saints. The views expressed herein are the responsibility of the author and do not necessarily represent the position of the Church.

THE EARTHQUAKE

Car crushed by the weight of the adobe walls.

Photo of Patzún, Guatemala, before the earthquake in 1976

MISSIONARIES IN COMALAPA

Elder Larry Richman.

I was a missionary serving in the Guatemalan town of Comalapa. My missionary companion, Elder Gary Larson, had joined several other missionaries in the nearby town of Patzicía to learn the Cakchiquel language spoken by the people in this area. I stayed in Comalapa to do missionary work with Eber Caranza, a 19-year-old member of the Church from the nearby town of Patzún. Tuesday night after a full day of missionary work, we went to bed expecting a good night's rest.

At 3:03:33am, Wednesday, February 4, 1976, Mother Earth let all hell break loose with a 45-second earthquake that measured 7.6 on the Richter scale (90 times stronger than the earthquake that leveled Managua, Nicaragua in 1972). The wall by the side of my bed gave way and about 200 pounds of adobe covered my bed, waking me from my sound sleep.

Inside our apartment in Comalapa after the quake. Eber's bed is on the left. My bed is on the right. (The red blanket at the foot of my bed is barely visible. The ceiling caved in after we left the room.)

At first, I thought it was a dream. I couldn't believe that I was actually lying in bed trapped, unable to move my arms or legs. The earth continued its horrible convulsions, and more dirt began to fill my face. This made me quickly realize that it wasn't a dream, and that if I was to live through this, I must get out fast! I soon freed one hand and with it pushed away the dirt that had covered my face. I thrust my hand upward waving it frantically and shouting for help.

Eber yelled back from the other side of the room. I pushed and finally freed myself from the blankets that held me prisoner and slid out on the side of the bed that wasn't covered with adobe. I looked in his direction and could see him faintly with the moonlight shining through the hole left by the fallen wall on the other side of the room. We found each other, and hand in hand we scrambled for the exit, climbing over his bed and out the hole in the wall.

View from the inner patio. The pink wall on the right is the outside wall of our room. On the far right are white doors that were jammed shut, so we crawled out the hole in the wall next to the doors to escape to the inner patio. The green room on the far left is the neighbor's kitchen; their wall having fallen into our patio.

Once outside of our room, we ran along the covered walkway (to the right in the picture), then down the steps into the garden. The earth began shaking again and caused us to fall several times before reaching the garden. Behind us, we could hear walls giving way and the roof crashing in.

We ran for the largest tree in the patio and held tight to its trunk. When the earth stopped shaking, it was deadly silent. We shook our heads, dazed by it all, and still wondering if we were dreaming or if this could be reality. Then out of silence we heard a distant rumble which grew ever louder as if a freight train was headed our way. What approached was much more destructive than a freight train. The earth began shaking again violently and the rumble grew to an almost deafening roar. Whatever was left standing after the first upheaval of the earth now came crashing down. The shaking stopped, the roar quieted to a rumble, then the rumble hushed to silence.

There we stood in the garden in our pajamas with bare feet in the wet grass, shaking from the cold and from fright. High adobe walls surrounded the garden, and the fallen house blocked our way to the street. We couldn't leave the garden, nor dared we. There was a deep ravine just a block from our house and with each succeeding tremor, we could hear more of the cliff around it cave in. See map.

Neighbors near and far began crying over dead husbands, wives, children, and parents. And for the next hour, over the moaning, we could hear the blood-chilling sound of someone chopping away at a large wooden post that pinned his loved one.

When it finally got light enough to see (about 5:30am), we carefully approached the house to grab pants and shoes and find a way out to the street.

Larry Richman about 3 hours after the quake, standing in front of Walter Matzer's room (our landlord), two doors down from our room.

Eber in front of our room in Comalapa reenacting how we quickly grabbed clothes and went out into the street. I am taking the picture standing in the street while my companion, Eber Caranza, stands in front of our room. The calendar hanging on the pink wall was at the head of my bed.

MEMBERS IN COMALAPA

As soon as we dressed, we headed straight for the home of the Miza family. On the way, we passed countless people who called to us for help or sympathy. When we arrived at the Miza's home, we were grateful to find them safe. The Miza family had been baptized just 12 days earlier as the first members of the Church in the town. (Learn more about the Miza family on the Comalapa page.) They stumbled out of bed and knelt in prayer in the center of the room as the house shook. The heavy adobe walls fell in all around them but none of the family was injured.

The Miza Family (Elena, Rigoberto, Hugo, and Noe) standing in front of their house after all the rubble had been removed.

Car crushed by the weight of the adobe walls.

Store front in Comalapa, days later

Comalapa (Photo courtesy Michael Morris)

GATHERING AND ORGANIZING OUR FORCES

While at the Miza's home, someone made an announcement over a loudspeaker asking everyone to remain calm and gather in the central plaza to organize ourselves to take care of the things we needed. Since there were 3,200 to 3,500 dead of the town's population of 20,000, crews were organized to handle the burials.

Other crews were organized to look into sources of food and clean water. However, the most immediate need was for medical help, since there were 5,000 people injured—many of whom needed immediate medical care—and not one doctor or nurse in town. (Doctors and nurses at the medical clinic had just left town and their replacements hadn't yet arrived.)

Since quakes follow along fault lines, I realized that there could be a nearby town that had not been hit as hard as Comalapa, and perhaps they could offer us medical aid. We felt that the most useful thing we could do was to offer to go to another town to try to get aid. Being that the mayor and his family were buried alive in their house, there was a bit of confusion, but we finally got a letter from the acting mayor asking the governor in Chimaltenango for help.

HEADING OUT OF COMALAPA

Since we could not find a horse or a motorcycle, we headed out on foot about 9:30am. The road out of Comalapa winds along the side of the mountain, and the shoulders give way to steep cliffs that descend hundreds of yards. As we walked along, there were still many tremors, and parts of the dirt road would break off and slide down the cliffs. About 10:00am, we met up with a couple who were also headed to Chimaltenango to find their son, so we traveled with them. On the way, we passed a few people heading into Comalapa and heard from them that the surrounding towns had been almost destroyed as well. We also heard reports that a missionary had died in Patzicía.

As we were walking out of Comalapa, parts of the road were still breaking off and sliding down the cliffs.

We walked or ran the whole way except for the last few miles when we got a ride in a jeep that had tried to make it to Comalapa but was forced to turn back because the road was impassable.

At noon, we arrived at the town of Zaragoza. From there, it was one direction to Chimaltenango and the opposite direction to Patzún, Eber's hometown. Since it appeared that Chimaltenango would not be able to offer us any aid, we decided to go to Patzún so Eber could find out about his family. We gave the letter from the acting mayor to the couple we were traveling with so they could deliver it to the governor in Chimaltenango. From Zaragoza, we walked another few miles before we got another ride that took us as far as the town of Patzicía. Our hearts sunk as we neared the church in Patzicía and found it almost destroyed.

PATZICÍA CHURCH

The Church of Jesus Christ of Latter-day Saints in Patzicía is visible from the highway. As we approached it, we could see that the church made of cement beams and cinderblock was destroyed. Although the classrooms along the side of the building were still standing, the roof over the chapel and the cultural hall had collapsed to the ground.

Patzicía church before the earthquake

Patzicía chapel after the earthquake

Patzicía chapel after the earthquake

Church in Patzicía from the cover of the Church News. Quotes below are from that article.

Church in Patzicía, Guatemala, after earthquake in 1976

Church in Patzicía, Guatemala after earthquake in 1976

"The quake caused the Patzicía chapel roof to slide backward about three feet, thus tipping over the massive reinforced concrete beams that supported it. As these beams toppled on their sides, their own weight was too great and they broke in the middle, dropping the roof in two nearly intact pieces into a V-shape. The only area standing is the classroom wing on the north. This, also, is heavily damaged." Read more details in these articles in the *Church News*.

Inside the chapel, looking toward the left side of the podium. The beam stopped just short of crushing the piano.

Inside the chapel, looking toward the right side of the podium.

Crushed benches in the chapel

Cultural hall, looking back at the left side of the stage

Another photo of the cultural hall, looking back at the left side of the stage

Cultural hall, looking back at the right side of the stage

Back of the church and covered walkway to the restrooms.

Back of the church in Patzicía, Guatemala after the earthquake of 1976 (Photo courtesy Michael Morris)

Missionaries in Patzicía

Senior Agricultural Missionary Couple

Elder Bleak Powell and Sister Gladys Powell in a native blouse and skirt in 1975 by the church in Patzicía, Guatemala before the earthquake.

Elder Bleak Powell and Sister Gladys Powell were agricultural missionaries, living in one of the classrooms at the church. Of their experience, Sister Powell wrote: "Around three o'clock in the morning we were awakened by the shaking of our bed…. The shaking became more violent…unbelievably violent! We could only try to hold on to the bed. We could hear the furniture and our personal belongings being thrown about the room. It was as if a huge giant had the chapel in his hands and was angrily shaking it. Suddenly we could hear the building breaking and crashing over us! The noise was deafening. Then the horrible shaking stopped, almost as abruptly as it had started. We stumbled out of bed and over the rubble and into the hall. Then we saw the grotesque pile that once had been the chapel and recreational room...the whole opposite side of the church had fallen!" (Excerpts from *February 4, 1976: We Were There*, an unpublished account by Gladys Powell.)

View from the back of the Patzicía church. The Powell's room was in the back right corner of the building.

Back of the church. (Photo by Dennis Atkin)

Sister Powell wrote: "As long as I live I shall never forget the sounds that began to arise from the people. We could hear the wailing and weeping as the people began to pull their families from under the piles of fallen adobe. Their homes were deathtraps, for the adobe was only mud and crumbled to crush and smother them. When daylight came, I could see that the home of our next-door neighbors was destroyed and I could hear the weeping of the women, so I climbed over the mounds of rubble into what had been their yard. Their little eight- or nine-year-old boy was walking around in a daze, carrying the body of his little dead sister in his arms. I put my arms around the mother and tried in my feeble way to comfort her, telling her that we have to be strong when things seem hopeless and that we have to have faith. She thanked me and softly said, 'It is God's will.'

"Many of the Indian brothers started coming to see if we were safe. One said, 'Sister, President Choc's wife and two little sons were killed.' Another came saying that the Relief Society President and her baby were dead." (Excerpts from *February 4,*

1976: We Were There, an unpublished account by Gladys Powell.)

ELDERS IN THE LANGUAGE CLASS

Several missionaries had been staying at the church taking the Cakchiquel language classes I mentioned earlier.

Elders Gary Larson, Steven Schmollinger, and Fred Bernhardt had been sleeping in an adobe house just outside the fence of the church grounds. They were spared injury because the walls of the house fell outward, and the gabled roof fell over their beds.

House where Elders Larson, Schmollinger, and Bernhardt were sleeping.

Inside the house where the missionaries were sleeping.

Elder Gary W. Larson

Elder Steven Schmolinger

Elder Fred Bernhardt (years later)

However, two other missionaries, Elders Randy Ellsworth and Dennis Atkin, had slept that night on mattresses on the stage in the cultural hall of the building.

Elder Randy Ellsworth and his wife, Sylvia (years later)

Elder Dennis Atkin and his wife, Beverly (years later, in 2002)

During the earthquake, the roof of the church building gave way, and one of the 60-ton concrete and steel beams descended and landed on Elder Ellsworth's back, pinning him to the wooden stage. Another beam fell on Elder Atkin's pillow, but fortunately the violent shaking had thrown him from the mattress, and he escaped injury.

Stage at the Patzicía church where Elder Ellsworth was pinned. See another photo and another.

These missionaries, along with members who arrived later, worked heroically through the black of night to free Elder Ellsworth. Unable to lift the beam, they spent six hours with crude tools cutting the stage floor beneath him. When more tremors came and bricks began to fall around them, Elders Evans and Salazar blessed the walls that they would not fall until Elder Ellsworth was rescued.

When they extracted Elder Ellsworth at about 9:00am or 9:30am, they put him in the bed of the Powells' small pickup and headed for the hospital in Guatemala City. Eber and I arrived in Patzicía about half an hour after the pickup left for Guatemala City. Elder Ellsworth was later flown to a hospital in Panama City, and then to the United States (see article 1 and 2) where one miracle after another saved his life and his legs. Six months later, he later returned to Guatemala to complete his mission. Read "I'll Stand and Preach the Gospel."

See [letter by President O'Donnal explaining Randy Ellsworth's story](#).

See the following talks in General Conference that relate information about Elder Ellsworth's experiences:

- Thomas S. Monson, [*Ensign*, Nov. 1976, page 53](#)
- Marion G. Romney, [*Ensign*, Nov. 1977, page 42](#)
- Thomas S. Monson, [*Ensign*, Nov. 1986, pages 41-42](#)

In a letter to President John O'Donnal 21 years after the ordeal, Randy Ellsworth wrote the following: "I feel I owe a great debt to the people of Guatemala and the missionaries who sacrificed so much in risking their own lives to save my life…. I am always given the credit for what happened in the earthquake, but in reality, I only awakened to find that a beam had fallen on me. It was the other missionaries and the brothers of Patzicía that, being safe and sound, risked their lives crawling to where I was, sure that I was going to die regardless. When a second tremor came, without hesitation, one of them raised his arm to the square using the Melchizedek Priesthood, blessed the walls that they would not fall until I was rescued. They are the ones who deserve the credit and I do not want to betray them. For me the elders and the brothers of Patzicía are the true heroes." ([*Pioneer in Guatemala: The Personal History of John Forres O'Donnal*](#), Shumway Family History Services, Yorba Linda, CA, pp. 130-1.)

LANGUAGE TEACHERS

Julio Salazar of Guatemala City

Julio Salazar (years later in 2016)

Taz Evans of Safford, Arizona

Elders Salazar and Evans, the language teachers, were living in the missionary quarters in the center of town. Elder Taz

Evans wrote the following: "The moment the earthquake hit, we were snatched from our beds and pulled outside. There is no doubt that it was a miracle and that we were removed from the house before any danger could befall us. Outside we knelt and had prayer, taking turns to pray aloud. We blessed the walls of our fallen room by the power of the priesthood, then crawled back to search for our flashlights and to get some clothes before running out to see what we could do." (*[Pioneer in Guatemala: The Personal History of John Forres O'Donnal](#)*, Shumway Family History Services, Yorba Linda, CA, p. 148.)

The elders made their way to the church and assisted in the heroic efforts to free Elder Ellsworth.

MISSIONARIES IN SUMPANGO

Elder Daniel Choc

Elder David Lee Frischknecht, of Ogden, Utah

"Elder Daniel Choc, son of Pablo Choc, and Elder David Frischknecht were in Sumpango. Every home on their street was a mass of rubble, except theirs. It held, and the elders were not injured." *(Church News)*

MISSIONARIES IN PATZÚN

The missionaries in Patzún were Elder Garth Howard and Elder Luis Manuel Argueta.

Elder Garth Howard, photo March 18, 1975

Elder Luis Manuel Argueta

22 MEMBERS KILLED — 15 IN PATZICÍA

Patzicía streets

Patzicía homes

LATTER-DAY SAINT MISSIONARIES IN THE 1976 GUATEMALA EARTHQUAKE

Elders Argueta and Richman in Patzicía

Patzicía, Guatemala days after the earthquake of 1976 (Photo courtesy of Michael Morris)

Patzicía, Guatemala, days after the earthquake of 1976. Elder Frischknecht on the left (Photo courtesy Michael Morris). See more street scenes: 1 and 2

Shoe shop

Fifteen members died in Patzicía, including the pregnant wife and two of the smaller sons of Pablo Choc, president of the Patzicía Branch. "Most of the members died in the rubble of their homes in the villages of Chimaltenango and Patzicía, about 40 miles north of Guatemala City. Most of the homes destroyed were small, adobe houses. With the first hard quake, they collapsed on the sleeping families taking a heavy death toll." *(Church News)*

Pablo Choc family before the earthquake at Elder Daniel Choc's missionary farewell. See alternate photos 1, 2, and 3.

The remains of Pablo Choc's home after the quake. All that is standing is the gate amidst the fallen outer wall.

It wasn't just adobe that came tumbling down. The Catholic cathedral made of brick and mortar in the town square in Patzicía was also broken into pieces.

Cathedral in the Patzicía town square. See alternate picture 1 and 2.

Elder Richman sitting on the remains of the brick-and-mortar tower of the cathedral in the town square in Patzicía, Guatemala.

Cathedral in the Patzicía, Guatemala town square days after the earthquake of 1976 (Photo courtesy of Michael Morris)

CONTINUING TO PATZÚN

Eber and I continued to Patzún to see his family. Just outside Patzicía, we got a ride in a truck that took us a few miles until the road became impassable. We then walked until the road became impassable even on foot. Since Eber grew up in the area, he knew of a trail through the woods, so we backtracked until we found the trail and took it to Patzún.

When we arrived in Patzún, we found about the same devastation as in the other towns but found that Eber's family was all right.

Photo of the municipal building in Patzún taken days later, after the rubble on the street had been cleared. Elder Daniel Choc is standing in front.

Elder Howard, Eber's sister, Eber's mother, Eber Caranza, and Eber's stepfather in Patzún.

I left Eber with his family and spent the night in Patzún with Elder Kelly Robbins and Elder D Warnock. Since we didn't want to sleep near any buildings, we slept on the hillside just above the house where the missionaries lived. There were tremors throughout the night, and we got very little rest.

Elder Kelly Robbins

Elder D Warnock, photo March 19, 1975

RETURNING TO PATZICÍA

Thursday morning, February 5, we returned to Patzicía. I admired the courage of Branch President Pablo Choc, who bore the responsibility for 325 members—some of whom died, many of whom were injured, and all of whom were left homeless. The branch Relief Society president Arcadia Miculax was dead. Pablo's pregnant wife was killed in the earthquake along with two sons. He was left to care for seven children, the oldest of which was Elder Daniel Choc Xicay, a missionary then serving in the nearby town Sumpango. That morning, we buried President Choc's wife, his two sons, and twelve other members of the branch in a single large grave. I dedicated the grave at President Choc's request.

Carrying members to the Patzicía cemetery.

Burying members at the Patzicía cemetery, February 4, 1976.

That night, our mission president Robert B. Arnold came with rolls of heavy plastic to cover our sleeping bags and make temporary lean-tos for the members as temporary shelters.

Sleeping outdoors by the Patzicía church.

President Arnold instructed us that our primary responsibility was to help the members with their immediate needs, and he asked me to stay in Patzicía. I was glad to be of service to the members in Patzicía, since I had worked in the town for almost nine months previously and knew the members well. Nevertheless, I felt a responsibility toward the town of Comalapa where I was assigned at the time of the earthquake. There was only one member family, and they were all right, but I felt that the rest of the town also needed our help and might feel that we had deserted them.

RETURNING TO COMALAPA

Friday morning, February 6, we returned to Comalapa to get our personal belongings since the wall in our room had fallen in the earthquake and the room was exposed to the street. By then, the road into town had been cleared and in places they had cut new roads through farmers' fields. We found that there was even more destruction in Comalapa than there had been at 9:30 the morning after the earthquake when we had left the town, since more had fallen during the tremors Wednesday and

Thursday. I wondered if the town would be rebuilt or if it would turn into a ghost town.

Elder Richman and Elder Larson cleaning out the missionary room in Comalapa

At our house in Comalapa, we found a note left by the zone leader, Elder Kirt Harmon. Read a story by Elder Kirt Harmon, published in the January 1979 *Ensign* that explains how he and Elder Daniel Choc went to Comalapa to check on us. (See a PDF of the story.)

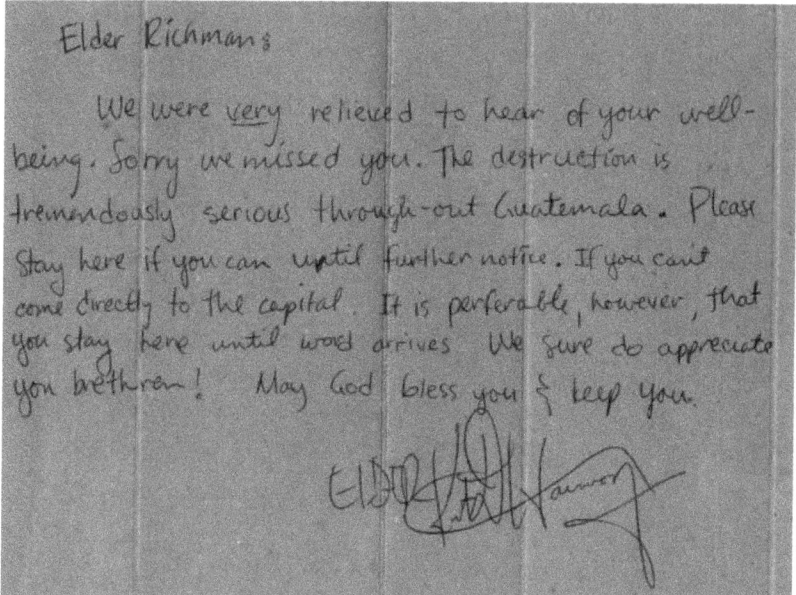

Note from the zone leaders.

CONCERN FROM PARENTS

It was many days before I could get word to my parents that I was all right. The day of the earthquake, my parents were able to talk with President Arnold's wife on the phone, and she assured them I was all right (even though the mission home had not yet been able to contact us). Nevertheless, my parents were anxious to hear from me to be sure. Dad sent five letters until he finally received one from me. The following is an excerpt from his letter dated Sunday, February 8, 1976:

> Dear Larry,
> These have been most anxious days for us this past week, watching the news and searching the newspaper. Our prayers are with you and your loved ones there. We pray for your welfare. We wish we could help. It was a relief to talk to the wife of your mission president, Sister Arnold, and she assured me you were okay, as well as Elder Luis Manuel Argueta. We know that this must be a heart-rendering experience for you as you help God's children

and as you exercise your priesthood, that many testimonies will grow, including your own. Our thoughts and our prayers are for you constantly. We know how much you love the people there.

We are still anxiously awaiting word from you. We pray that you are getting enough to eat and water to drink. We hear all kinds of stories of starvation and epidemic conditions. As soon as you can, write, telegram, or call us. We love you so much and know that you are really busy. Please let us know how you are as soon as you can. We pray that all of our Father's choicest blessings will be with you and the members there.

All our love, Dad

On February 16, he wrote, "We hope you are well and that things are starting to get back to normal. We are still anxiously awaiting word from you. Please call, telegram, or write and let us know how you are." (The last letter he had received from me was January 27.)

I couldn't call or telegram, because the lines weren't functioning. The following two letters dated February 11, 1976, are two of many letters I wrote home, hoping that at least one of them would make it.

2-11-76

Dear Family,

Just a note to let you know that I'm ok. I'm sending two letters, hoping that for sure one of them gets to you.

The Lord has saved us all from the earthquake. All the missionaries are alive & only one was seriously hurt. He looks like he'll be ok. Now he's in Washington, DC in an Army Hospital. I escaped without any injury even though our house fell down. Almost everything in this area came tumbling down in the few seconds initial earthquake & the succeeding tremors. As I am writing this letter, I just felt a small tremor. They continue & will do so for a few more weeks. But don't worry because the Lord is protecting His missionaries. He has done so far & will continue to do so. Of that I have great faith.

So tell all the relatives that I'm ok! I won't have much time to write because we are very busy supplying all the members with food, water, medicine, blankets, tents, etc. After which will be a gigantic re-construction program. Please save all the newspaper articles. I'll write whenever I get a chance. Don't worry about anything. The Lord's watching over us.

Love Always,
Larry

write to:
Apartado 2369
Guate, Guate.

Letter home February 11, 1976.

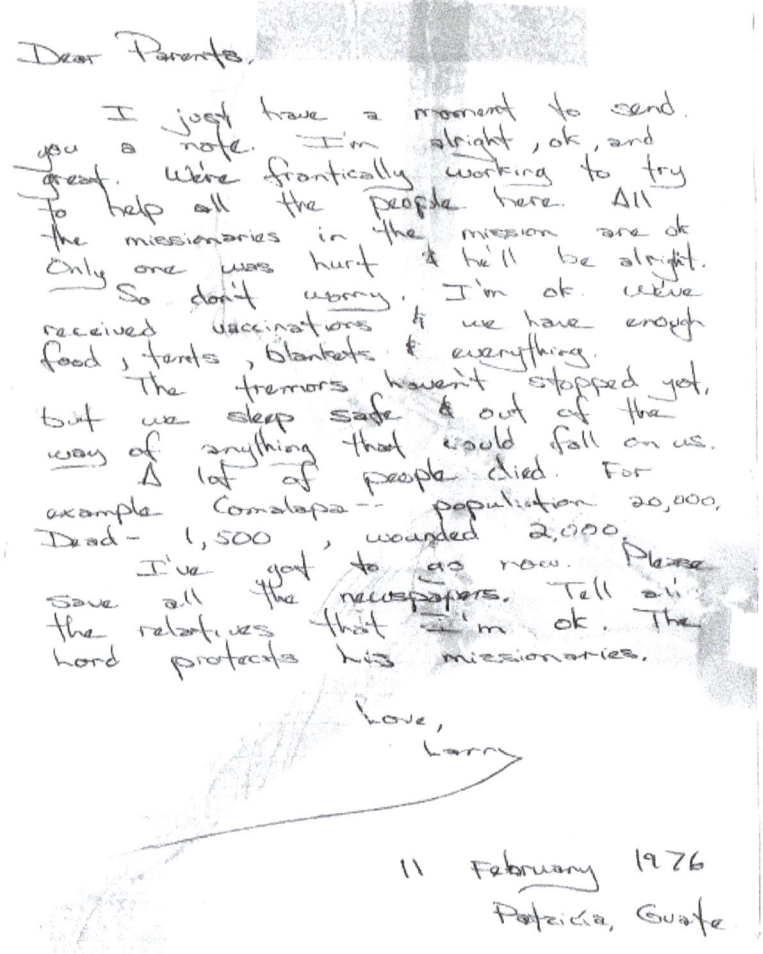

Another letter home February 11, 1976.

One of these letters arrived in Boise on February 17. Dad wrote me back the next day, saying "We received your letter yesterday dated Feb 11th. You don't know how relieved we are to hear all is well with you. We know our Father in Heaven is protecting you, but we were still anxious to hear from you."

Read an article from the Idaho Statesman newspaper about the earthquake and a report on Elder Richman.

RELIEF CAME QUICKLY

Missionaries assisted in distributing food, clothing, and blankets, as well as pots and pans for cooking and boiling water. Doctors and health missionaries arrived to give injections to prevent hepatitis and typhoid. We feared widespread epidemics because of the contaminated water supplies and because they were still digging dead bodies out of the rubble several days after the earthquake. The stake in Quetzaltenango immediately sent carloads of supplies, and soon additional help arrived from the Church in Salt Lake.

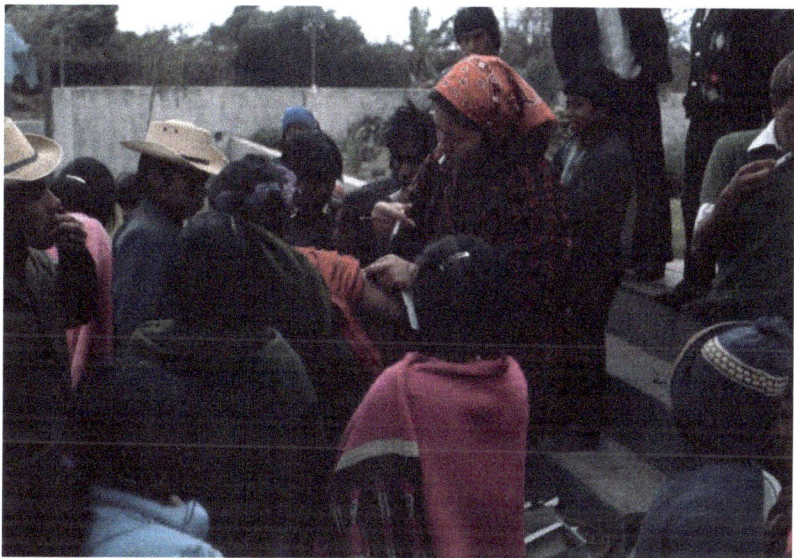

Sister Cathy Hyer gives injections of Gamma Globulin and typhoid vaccine to people to prevent widespread disease.

Elder Richman assists.

People began to clear out the rubble with their hands and hoes. Within a few days, big machinery arrived to begin to clear the streets.

Clearing the streets in Comalapa days later (Photo courtesy of Michael Gre)

WORK CAMP PATZICÍA

We set up a camp of tents around the church building in Patzicía and sixteen missionaries spent the next two months in jeans and t-shirts working with shovels and picks helping the people clear out their home sites to make way to build new houses. We were anxious to get the members into houses before the rainy season began in just a few months. We hauled away the old adobe bricks, took apart the roofs, and stacked the timbers and corrugated metal sheets.

Sundays were spent in church and other meetings to organize work parties, but the other six days a week we left camp at 6:30am and returned dusty and dirty at 5:00pm. We would then bathe, eat, and go to bed. One morning, for example, three of us worked at a man's house carrying 35-pound adobe bricks on our shoulders from the house, 110 feet to the road where we dumped them. During the five hours we were at his house, we moved about 32,000 pounds. One missionary commented that in all the years bucking hay on his dad's farm, he had never worked harder in his life than he did that day. We didn't look for praise from our parents or from the mission president; we worked because we loved the people and wanted to help them.

How to tear down an adobe wall: Step 1. Elder Larson and Elder Richman chipping the plaster off a wall.

How to tear down an adobe wall: Step 2. Elder Richman and others push over an adobe wall.

Elder Richman pushing over a wall

Tearing down a wall during a work day in Sumpango, March 1, 1976

And the wall came down

Elders Bernhardt and Richman stack wood after dismantling a roof in Sumpango

Elder Gary Larson in Sumpango

Elders Richman and Gibson after a work day in Sumpango.

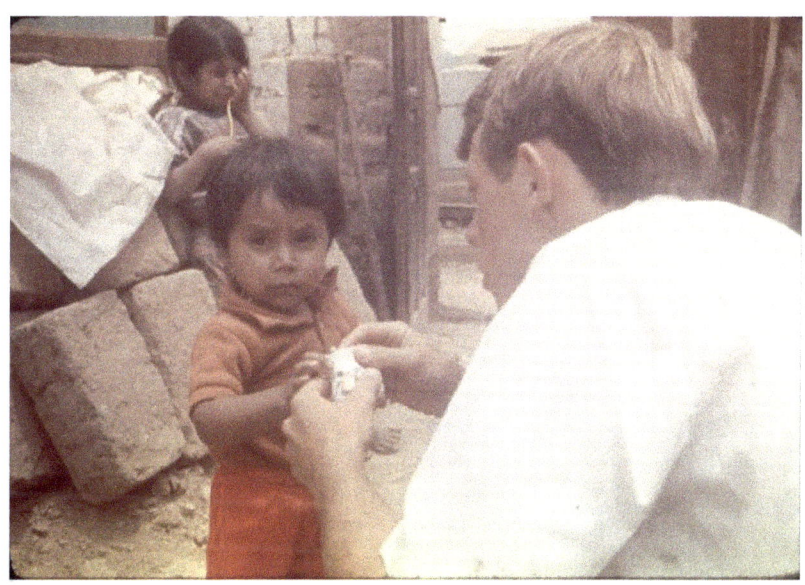

Elder Richman helping a child

Elder Richman in Sumpango.

Elder Atkin is on the right

Elder Warnock (on the left) and Elder Larson (on the right) tear down damaged walls after the earthquake in Guatemala 1976

Tearing down a wall

Each preparation day (Monday) for two months after the earthquake, the Guatemala City Zone and the Quetzaltenango Zone joined us to work in mass in a town to help members and nonmembers alike. Read about the missionaries working in towns on their preparation days in the article "Elders Help Rebuild Guatemala" from the *Church News*.

Missionary work day in Comalapa, February 23, 1976

Missionary work day in Comalapa, February 23, 1976

Work day in Comalapa February 23, 1976

Comalapa street

Street scene in Comalapa looking from the park

Street view in Comalapa looking from the Calvario

Elder Bernhardt sitting on a rock next to a dead chicken after the work day in Comalapa

DIARIO LA TARDE

No. 1644 — Director General: Jorge Carpio Nicolle
Guatemala, sábado 28 de febrero de 1976. — Año VI

LOS MORMONES MUEVEN MONTAÑAS

EN PREPARACION para un día de trabajo duro, misioneros de todas partes de Guatemala empiezan a dividirse en cuadrillas de trabajadores.

Como sorpresa al pueblo de Comalapa, Chimaltenango, el día lunes 23 de febrero, un grupo de más de 100 misioneros de la Iglesia de Jesucristo de los Santos de los Últimos Días llegaron en dos camionetas, una de la capital y la otra de Quezaltenango, con el propósito de demostrar y reconstruir una parte del pueblo.

Bajo la dirección de Boyce Lines y Bleak Powell, misioneros de agricultura de la Iglesia, la cuadrilla se dividió en grupos de cinco y seis obreros. Cada grupo recibió las herramientas necesarias y fueron asignados para dar servicio a familias específicas bajo la instrucción del hermano Rigoberto Misa Moxó, quien se convirtió a la Iglesia Mormona en Comalapa hace un mes.

A las nueve horas, comenzaron la labor larga y pesada de limpieza y restauración de lo que quedó del pueblito después de la tragedia que nos sucedió el 4 de los corrientes.

Los misioneros lograron desmontar completamente unos 18 lotes pertenecientes a familias no miembros de la Iglesia, dejando que los tractores municipales quiten el desperdicio de las casas caídas sin hacer daño a los pisos que quedaron intactos.

Missionaries stopping for a watermelon break on the road out of Comalapa after the work day. (Elders Evans, Choc, and Frischknecht in foreground)

We (about 4 elders) went to Guatemala City on February 23, 1976, after the Comalapa work day and spent the night in the Ritz Continental Hotel, 6a Avenida "A" 10-13 in zone 1. The hotel was not badly damaged by the earthquake. It was strange to sleep again indoors, worried that heavy walls might fall on us during one of the tremors that were still occurring.

Helicopter delivering aid in the Comalapa town square

Comalapa town square several months later. (Photo courtesy of Michael Morris)

In 2009, showing the facade of the old Comalapa Catholic church rebuilt and a new church beside it.

Four camp studs: Garth Howard, Kelly Robbins, Lance Standifird, Larry Richman

Elders Daniel Choc, Julio Salazar, and Dennis Atkin

Elder and Sister Boyce and Carol Lines helped supervise the camp.

Elder Bleak Powel and Elder Luis Manuel Argueta

Bleak Powell, David Frischknecht, Garth Howard, Cleo Fromm, Kelly Robbins, Hye Fromm

Hye and Cleo Fromm helped supervise the camp

Hye and Cleo Fromm

Elder Richman beginning a day's work

Elders Argueta and Richman on the street in Patzicía, Guatemala

In Patzicía. Only the doors of this house are still standing

Elders Richman and Argueta

Elder Argueta is on the right

Elder Argueta

Elder Richman

Elders Argueta and Richman behind the Patzicía church. See alternate photo.

Work crew 1: Elders Bernhardt, Salazar, Richman, and Schmolinger

Work crew 2: Elders Choc, Larson, Frischknecht, and Evans

Elders Richman, Salazar, Choc, Evans, Larson, Frischknecht, and Bernhardt

Camp Patzicía workers

The "Camp Patzicía crew"

LATTER-DAY SAINT MISSIONARIES IN THE 1976 GUATEMALA EARTHQUAKE

The "Camp Patzicía" crew. See the page [Where are they today?](#)

Elder Wait, Elder Worthington, Elder Bernhardt, Sister Powell, Brother Powell, Elder Howard, Sister Sharp, Elder Schmolinger, Sister Hyer, and Elder Warnock.

Mixing adobe mud. Elders Larson, Robbins, and Richman

A busload of help arrives in Patzicía from the USA

Elder Argueta's mother arrives with help.

For part of the two months of Camp Patzicía, another missionary and I took care of the camp during the day. One day for example, we saw a calf born, killed six chickens, hauled several hundred gallons of water up from the well, distributed food and clothing to people who showed up at the church, washed the morning and evening dishes, cleaned the kitchen, dining room, tents, and camp, sorted the clean clothing and delivered it to each tent, ran some errands in town, and moved a piano and some other things from the rooms in the church.

One day when Greg Martin and I were in the camp, a helicopter landed in the field next to the church. A man came running out of the helicopter and asked, "Did you get the powdered milk from Canada?" It seemed an odd question, since we didn't know anything about milk from Canada.

Elder Richman washing clothes

Sister Cathy Hyer and Sister Geraldine Pullam

LATTER-DAY SAINT MISSIONARIES IN THE 1976 GUATEMALA EARTHQUAKE

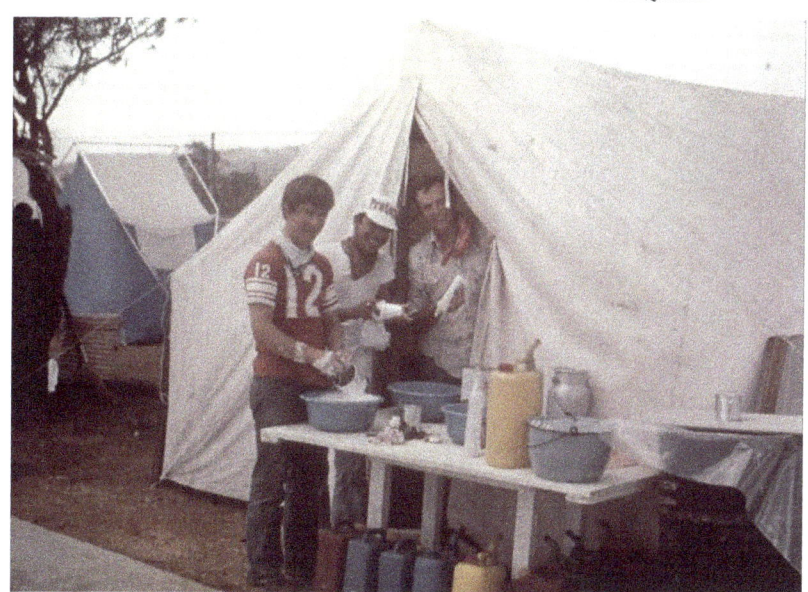

Elders Howard, Argueta, and Robbins washing up after a day of work

Garth Howard, Kelly Robbins, Cathy Hyer

Enjoying a free moment to celebrate Elder Kelly Robbins' birthday. Elders Howard, Robbins, Argueta

Elder Kelly Robbins' birthday. Elder Howard, Sister Johnson, Sister Wheatly, Elder Robbins, and Elder Richman

We continued to have tremors several times a day. No one slept under anything heavier than paper, cardboard, or cloth.

We often wondered if a larger quake would come as they experienced in the town of Antigua many years ago. A quake knocked down buildings and killed people, but three weeks later an even larger quake hit which destroyed the town.

For a few weeks, the Guatemalan National Observatory installed a seismograph in town. It measured tremors of up to 3.5 on the Richter scale. They come from near the surface, which means the ground is moving and unstable. The center of the activity is about four miles south of Patzicía, near the volcano Fuego.

David Frischknecht and Julio Salazar

Elders Argueta and Richman

Back of the Patzicía church with Elder Argueta and Elder Choc

Elder Richman and Walter Matzer (our landlord in Comalapa) collecting sand at the river.

Sunday services outside in Patzicía, Guatemala for the first few weeks

Temporary church structure where meetings were held until the church was rebuilt.

Services inside the temporary church structure where meetings were held in Patzicía, Guatemala until the new chapel was rebuilt

Elders Richman and Argueta

Elder Larry Richman, work missionary

Elder Larry Richman and his tent companion, Elder Luis Manuel Argueta.

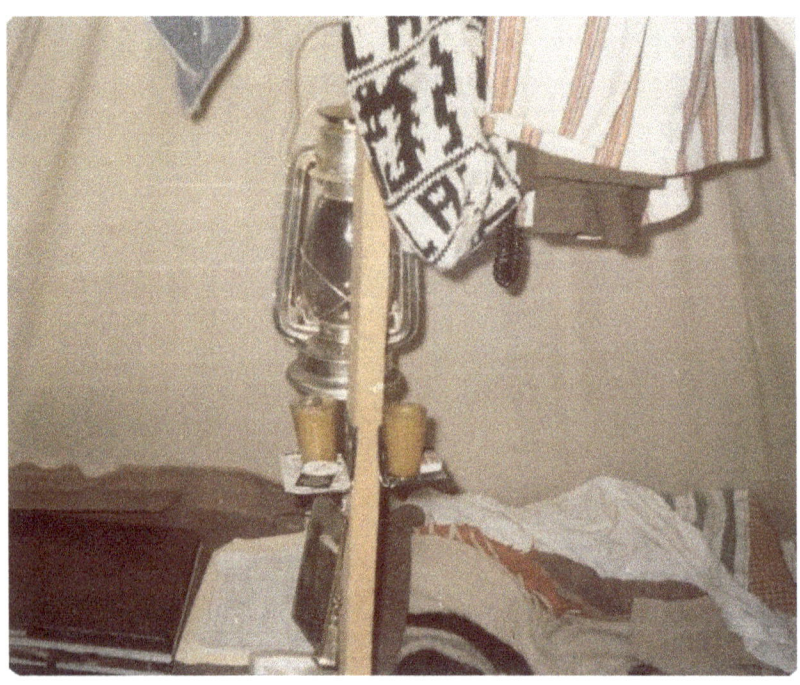

Inside our tent at Camp Patzicía

Sister Arcadia Miculax Secay (daughter of Mateo Miculax and Petronilia Secay) was the Relief Society president in Patzicía and she died in the earthquake, along with her baby Baudilio. Her husband, Ricardo Cua Itzol was not a member. But the urgency of the earthquake helped him decide to get baptized.

Elder Choc and Elder Salazar teaching Ricardo Cua

Elders Salazar and Choc preparing a spot for the baptism in the river Balanyá

Elder Salazar baptizing Ricardo Cua in the river Balanyá on February 12, 1976

Elder Choc baptizing in the river Balanyá on February 12, 1976

Elder Richman preparing to confirm Ricardo Cua a member of the Church on the banks of the river Balanyá on February 12, 1976.

Elder Richman confirming Ricardo Cua a member of the Church on the banks of the river Balanyá on February 12, 1976.

Brother Ricardo Cua later died in an accident while mixing pesticides. Elder Larry Richman and Elder David Frischknecht performed the temple work for him and his wife, Arcadia Miculax Xicay, on July 18, 1979. See the family genealogy sheets and letter about the temple work.

Making an adobe house with Brother Per

Making an adobe house, Elder Frischknecht and Elder Richman

President Robert B. Arnold in Patzún to discuss the housing reconstruction project with the members. (Also shown: Eber Caranza, Gary Larson, D Warnock).

Since most of the members had no financial means—no savings nor the ability to borrow money—to reconstruct homes, the Church developed a plan to help them.

Mission president Robert Arnold meeting with Patzún members

Signs like this printed on cardstock began appearing:

GUATEMALA ¡EN PIE!

Litografía José Arimany Hijos

¡Guatemala en pie!
("Guatemala is still standing!" or "Guatemala is still on its feet!")

JUNTEMOS NUESTRAS MANOS Y LEVANTEMOS A NUESTRO PUEBLO
COMALAPA VIVE

FAM. SALAZAR

Juntemos nuestras manos y levantemos a nuestro pueblo. Comalapa vive.
("Let's join our hands and raise our town. Comalapa lives.")

Con tu ayuda ¡Señor! reconstruiremos Comalapa.
("With thy help Lord, we will rebuild Comalapa.")

Postage stamps were later issued commemorating the earthquake

As mentioned previously, each Monday for two months after the earthquake, all the missionaries from several zones joined us to work in mass in a town to help people clean up and prepare for rebuilding. The last Monday of the camp was March 29, 1976, and we were working in the town of Patzún. After this, we were to break the work camp and go back to regular missionary work.

Work day in Patzún

Several missionaries were picking away at the bottom of a 15-foot wall (similar to the one pictured above) when it gave way prematurely and fell.

Everyone scrambled to safety, except for Elder Daniel Choc who was crushed by a four-foot section of brick and cement. Elder Warnock gave him artificial respiration while he was rushed to a nearby school that had been converted into a hospital. But the Lord soon called him home.

We thought we had seen the end of death from the earthquake two months before that, but now it took another life that was dear to us. All we could do was ask ourselves, "Why was it him under that wall and not me?" Despite the difficulties he had in his life, Elder Choc was always happy and was a good friend to us. He was also an asset to the mission, being the only native Cakchiquel missionary. He patiently taught us to understand his people and speak their language.

Daniel Choc Xicay

Pablo Choc family at Elder Daniel Choc's missionary farewell. See alternate photos 2 and 3

We put his dear body in a pickup truck, and Elder Boyce Lines, Elder D Warnock, Elder Julio Salazar, and I took him to Patzicía. The branch president Pablo Choc, Daniel's father, was at the Patzicía church when we arrived. President Choc had experienced nearly the tests of Job but remained strong and true. He and his wife had given birth to ten children, and she was expecting her eleventh when she died in the earthquake. Pablo was then left with six living children.

The mission president and I prepared Daniel's body and placed it in the casket. He was only about 5′ 2″, but he was a giant of a man in my eyes. We left on the lapel of his suit the button he wore which read "Por sacrificio se dan bendiciones" ("Blessings come through sacrifice").

Carrying Daniel Choc's coffin to the cemetery. Missionaries pictured (from left to right): Elder Fred Bernhardt, Elder David Frischknecht, Elder Kelly Robbins, Elder Julio Salazar, Fulgencio Choy, Jose Leon Choy, and Elder Garth Howard (front right of coffin).

President Robert B. Arnold and Pablo Choc at Daniel's funeral.

Pablo Choc at Daniel's funeral.

I can only imagine the feelings of a father who sent his son on a mission and then lost his wife and 3 children in the earthquake. I can only image the faith it took for him to be strong for his family—and for all the other members of the branch, who also lost family. Then I can only imagine the agony two months later, when he lost his missionary son in this accident.

Through all these tests, President Choc remained strong and true. He is one of the most noble, dignified, and humble men I know. He and his wife had given birth to ten children, and she was expecting her eleventh when she was killed in the earthquake. Pablo was then left with only six living children.

On January 24, 2007, Margaret Blair Young wrote: "Fulgencio Choy said that *many* people—in and out of the Church—watched Pablo Choc to see how he would respond to his tragedy [losing his wife and several children in the earthquake], and that his example of strength was one of main reasons the Church grew so beautifully in Patzicía. (10% of Patzicians are Latter-day Saints now—five wards, one stake, two additional branches in the aldeas.)"

The funeral services were held at Pablo Choc's home on March 30. (See the [funeral program](#).) I spoke about the six weeks we were companions in Comalapa. During those six weeks he taught me things that I thought I already knew—like what love is and what dedication and commitment are all about. One day, Elder Choc and I set a goal to teach ten discussions. As we knocked on doors to find those ten people to teach, and after being turned away at a door, Elder Choc would often run—not walk—to knock on the next door.

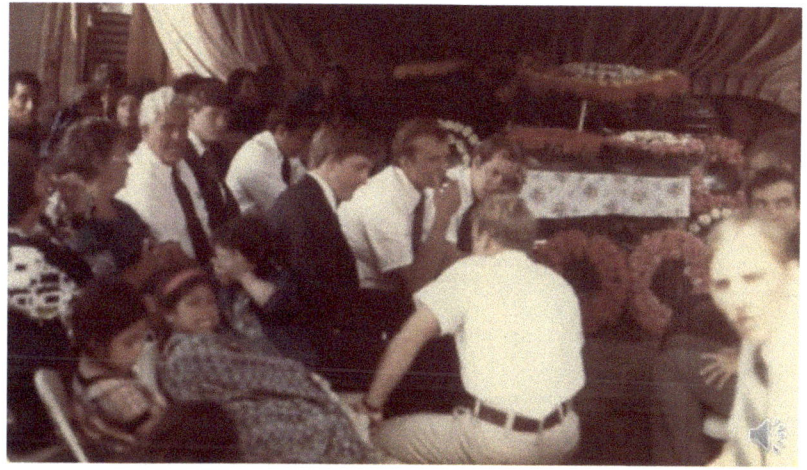

Elders Argueta, Richman, Robbins, and Larson at Daniel Choc's funeral

Elder Choc was deserving of two honors. He was the world's first Cakchiquel missionary, and now he is the first Cakchiquel missionary in the spirit world. In Doctrine and Covenants 138:57, we read of the vision given to President Joseph F. Smith about the spirit world: "I beheld that the faithful elders of this dispensation, when they depart from mortal life, continue their labors in the preaching of the gospel of repentance and redemption, through the sacrifice of the Only Begotten Son of God, among those who are in darkness and under the bondage of sin in the great world of the spirits of the dead."

Elder Choc's casket was placed in a tomb built over the grave of his mother, two brothers, and the twelve other members of the branch that we buried on February 5th. President Arnold dedicated the grave.

Elders Argueta, Larson, Robbins, and Richman at Daniel Choc's grave.
(See additional photo of Elder Gary Larson, Lynn Richman, and Elder Frischknecht by Elder Daniel Choc's grave in August 1976 when my parents came to pick me up from my mission.)

Elder Hixon at Daniel Choc's grave

Elder Daniel Choc's grave is to the left of the deud tree

Daniel Choc's headstone

On the front of his tomb is a marble headstone with the following inscription: "When ye are in the service of your fellow beings ye are only in the service of your God. Mosiah 2:17. Daniel Choc (Xicay). Born December 11, 1953. Died March 29, 1976. The first Cakchiquel missionary of The Church of Jesus Christ of Latter-day Saints who died serving his people."

Each of us took time to sit by the grave and record our thoughts. See photos of Elder Argueta, Elder Larson, and Elder Richman.

I look forward to the day when I pass through the veil and meet Elder Choc again with open arms, and I can thank him like I never really did in this life for his friendship and the example he showed me.

"It was impossible to get Elder Choc angry at you. You couldn't argue with him either." —Julio Salazar

"Elder Choc taught me through his example the true meaning of brotherly kindness, dedication, and consecration." —Larry Richman

Fulgencio Choy and Daniel Choc. Fulgencio's nickname was "colochin."

Elder Is Killed Clearing Debris Left by Quake

PATZICIA, GUATEMALA

The earthquake of February which killed so many people here has claimed another victim, adding to the burden of sorrow of Pres. Pablo Choc, president of the Patzicia Branch.

Pres. Choc lost his wife and two sons in the initial quake when their small home collapsed during the night of the quake.

A son, Elder Daniel Choc, the first Cakchiquel Indian missionary in the Church, was killed March 29 in the town of Patzun, when an adobe wall fell on him, according to Pres. Robert B. Arnold, president of the Guatemala Guatemala City Mission.

Elder Choc was working with 60 other missionaries on their "preparation day" helping clean up rubble in Patzun when the wall fell on him, killing him.

Pres. Choc has one son, Serapio, still living.

Newspaper article

"He died in the service of the Lord while doing missionary work—fellowshipping and helping a nonmember. What better way to die!" —President Robert B. Arnold

"I have had the privilege to interview Elder Choc and to know the intimate details of his life. I assure you that Elder Choc left this world completely dedicated and completely pure." —President Robert B. Arnold

"I just hope I'm in as good a shape when I die as Elder Choc was." —President Robert B. Arnold

See the following articles in Church magazines about Elder Daniel Choc:

- "The Dedicated Daniel Choc," *Ensign,* January 1979 (See PDF of the article). Read the article in Spanish (page 1, page 2, page 3).
- "Daniel Choc, First Cakchiquel Missionary," *New Era,* April 1978

See this telegram from Walter Matzer (our landlord in Comalapa).

Letter to Editor

Missionary's Death Prompts Tribute

Editor Herald:

It was with sorrow that I learned of the death March 29 of Elder Daniel Choc of Patzicia, Guatemala, a full-time missionary in the Guatemala Mission. He was crushed by an adobe wall which fell, as he and 60 other missionaries were helping clear away rubble in the earthquake-devastated town of Patzun.

I have seen no notice of his death in the local press, but feel that his passing deserves special tribute. He was an extraordinary missionary, and he and his family are known to many people in Utah.

The first Cakchiquel missionary in the Church, Elder Choc gave distinguished service during his year of labor in Patzun, Comalapa, Sumpango and Patzicia. He was loved and respected by his missionary companions and associates. Patiently he taught them to understand the Cakchiquel people and to speak the difficult Mayan dialect. From his own love and understanding of the native culture, he was able to communicate with great power and clarity the message that was so precious to him.

Prior to his mission, Daniel Choc had lived for two years with the Cordell Andersen family in Guatemala. It was there that he developed an appreciation of missionary work as he served a local mission among the Pocomchi Indians of Paradise Valley, baptising 24 and serving as a teacher among them.

Our brother, Daniel Choc, now joins his mother and two young brothers who were victims of the tragic earthquake that struck last February.

Daniel's father, Pablo Choc, president of the Patzicia Branch of the LDS Church, who has suffered such a loss, to Daniel's beautiful Indian sweetheart, to the Cordell Andersens, who held him as one of their own family and gave of themselves so unselfishly to bring out the greatness of this young man, to his missionary companions and members of the church who loved Daniel Choc and feel keenly his absence, I send my love and heartfelt sympathy.

May the memory of this remarkable saint and missionary be blessed, and may God raise up others to serve as he did.

Humbly submitted,
Robert Blair
Provo

Letter to the editor about Daniel Choc

Elder Choc's girlfriend, Feliza Choy, was an inspiration of strength. She later served a full-time mission.

Feliza Choy

Feliza Choy (Elder Daniel Choc's girlfriend) talking with Elder Argueta and Elder Richman

THE CONCLUSION OF CAMP PATZICÍA

Camp Patzicía ended on March 31, 1976, and the missionaries who worked there were assigned to return to proselyting work in various towns. Read where these missionaries are today.

Another group of 35 labor missionaries (local prospective full-time missionaries and BYU students) took over the tents and during a period of nine months, built over 250 small cinder block homes for the members. Read the article "Cementing Ties in Guatemala" *(New Era,* February 1977) about the workers who helped reconstruct homes. Also see "Rebuilding After Guatemala Quake."

Construction camp making cinderblocks

Construction camp crew

Tent city at the Patzicía church for the construction missionaries

Members help break up the roof at the Patzicía church

Demolition of the church in Patzicía, Guatemala

Demolition of the church in Patzicía, Guatemala

Clearing debris from the Patzicía church

I lived with the Cakchiquel people and saw them work and toil. I helped them build their houses with bright hopes for the future and then helped them shovel away the debris after those hopes were destroyed in a 45-second earthquake. I lived with them, prayed with them, sweated with them, and helped them bury their dead. I shared their joy when I saw success and progress.

For me the earthquake began as if a nightmare. I thought I was dreaming that I was trapped in bed. I thought I could wake up and everything would be all right. But I woke up to find the nightmare was a reality that shattered hopes and dreams. But the earthquake ended up being a cleansing of sorts. Towns have been rebuilt, new dreams have been born, and with a firm trust in God there is even more hope for a bright future.

Elena, Nelson, and Rigoberto Miza in their new home in July 1978

Children in Patzicía playing with construction materials at the rebuilding of the church in Patzicía in 1978

PABLO CHOC

Pablo Choc

Pablo Choc joined the Church in 1960, among the first indigenous Cakchiquel people to accept the restored gospel. Within a few short years, he was called as branch president. One of his tasks was to find a place to build a meetinghouse for the rapidly growing branch. He eventually purchased property, and, with supplies provided by the Church, branch members built the first meetinghouse in Patzicía. Choc was employed as the building's caretaker.

In 1966, Pablo and his wife, Augustina, were sealed in the Mesa Arizona Temple. After serving briefly as the district secretary, he was again called as branch president.

Passport photo of Daniel Choc's family when they went to the Mesa temple to be sealed.

Learn more about Pablo Choc:
- "[A 'David' in Stature, 'Goliath' in Gospel](#)" in the *Church News*.
- "[Un legado de fé y servicio en Patzicía](#)" on the Church's newsroom page for Guatemala
- "[Mi llamamiento me ayudó mucho](#)" (also in English, "[My Calling Helped Me a Lot](#)") in the global history collection on the Church site.

Pablo Choc tells about saving for years for Daniel to go on a full-time mission. He had saved 100-150 quetzals, which was a large sum of money in those days. One day, the military was in town to round up young men as potential recruits for the military. The way they "recruit" is to grab potential young men from the street and take them to the jail where they sort through those they want. Pablo had to give the guards the 100-150 quetzals to get Daniel freed, which left nothing for the mission. Other members and the mission came up with the needed money so that Daniel could serve, and missionaries donated clothing for Daniel to use.

Carlos Choc selling chickens in the market to support Daniel Choc's mission

Pablo Choc family at Elder Daniel Choc's missionary farewell, March 12, 1975.

Pablo Choc family and others at Elder Daniel Choc's missionary farewell, March 12, 1975. See alternate photos 2 and 3

Pablo Choc's daughters Magdelena and Florinda

Elder David Frischknecht with Magdelena, Florinda, and Rolando Choc

Austin and Cesar

Austin Choc 1977

Austin Choc, Elder David Frischknecht, and Cesar at the Calvario in Patzicía

On February 4, 1976, a catastrophic earthquake struck Guatemala. Patzicía was near the center of the devastation. Homes and other buildings throughout the city were leveled. Pablo's own home collapsed, and his pregnant wife and their two youngest children were killed. After digging out their bodies from the rubble, he was informed that the meetinghouse had collapsed, and a missionary was pinned beneath a massive roof beam.

The remains of Pablo Choc's home after the quake. All that is standing is the gate amidst the fallen outer wall.

Read how Pablo Choc responded to his duties as branch president on the pages <u>Latter-day Saint Missionaries in the Guatemala Earthquake of 1976</u> and <u>LDS Missionaries in the Guatemala Earthquake of 1976, Part 2</u>.

Sister Powell wrote: "Our dear Branch President Pablo Choc who lost his wife and two little sons in the quake goes about his duties with a smile on his face. But when we are alone and talking, he says, 'Oh, Hermana, I miss my wife so much. My home is so sad. I just hope that I can live worthy and work in the church so that I can be with them again. This life isn't too long. We just have to go on and do the best we can.' His son, Daniel, the first Cakchiquel Indian to go on a full-time mission came to our tent the other night. He is here with the other missionaries working. He said, 'I just can't believe that my mother is dead. It is so sad for me, but it is much sadder for my little sisters. They need her so much.' But he goes along each day in his missionary work laughing with the other missionaries. Perhaps they don't know the pain that is in his heart." (Excerpts from "February 4, 1976: We Were There," an unpublished account by Gladys Powell.)

Pablo Choc at Daniel's funeral.

President Pablo Choc was an inspiration. Many people, both members of the Church and those who weren't members, watched Pablo Choc to see how he would respond to these tragedies. His example of strength was an important reason the Church has grown so beautifully in Patzicía. In 1976, there was just one branch in Patzicía, and in 2015, there were four wards and a stake centered in Patzicía.

Pablo Choc family in 1977

First Stake Presidency in Patzicía

Pablo Choc in 2006. (Pablo Choc on the right. Margaret Blair Young in the center.)

Pablo Choc in 2006 with his daughter and granddaughter

"We may not know what contribution our small thread makes in the great tapestry. We may not understand the pattern that our lives make as they intersect, connect, separate, and intersect again, but God does."
-Chieko N. Okazaki

This is a swatch from a corte that has been in the Pablo Choc family for years. This swatch was prepared by Margaret Blair and given to missionaries who served in Patzicía during a missionary reunion at the Robert Blair home on October 2, 2015.

Pablo Choc and his wife

Pablo Choc's wife and child who died in the earthquake

Pablo Choc died July 28, 2010.

Learn more about the Pablo Choc family:

- See the <u>Patzicía page</u> for more photos and information about the Pablo Choc family.
- "<u>El CID y Ayuda</u>" (also in English, "<u>El CID and Ayuda</u>") in the global history collection on the Church site.

DANIEL CHOC

In the late 1960s, former missionaries who had served in Guatemala determined to alleviate the impact of the abject poverty they had witnessed throughout the country. They purchased a small farm in Valparaiso (near Cobán), where they established elementary and trade schools and built new, clean homes for local people. One of Pablo Choc's sons, Daniel Choc, was one of many teenagers who came from several areas to the Center for Indian Development ("El Centro Indígena de Desarrollo"), commonly called "El CID," to learn how to live, work, and have what was called "The Good Life." Later, Daniel's siblings, Serapio and Carmela, also worked at El CID.

The following is from the Guatemalan Foundation website:

"One of them from Patzicía, Daniel Choc, learned quickly and was the first to be taught how to operate the new Ford tractor and all its implements. This tractor was actually the first project of the Foundation in 1970. Daniel in the next 2 years taught 26 others, students and full-time employees how to also drive the tractor.

"After 2 years as a student and supervisor at The CID, he returned to his home in Patzicía. It was said in the LDS congregation there, 'Daniel left here a boy and returned a man.' He went on to become the first full-time LDS Cakchiquel missionary.

"It was Daniel who replied to the question of how best to help his people, replying, 'Formalize the program at Valparaiso and give other youth like me a chance to learn how to live and work.' He is given the credit for naming Valparaiso 'The Center for Indian Development.' Between him and Cordell the plan was, after his mission to establish in Patzicía 'The CID #2,' with Daniel as administrator, but tragically during his mission he was killed in the aftermath of the 1976 earthquake that killed 23,000 Guatemalans."

Read the story of Elder Daniel Choc Xicay as a missionary in Comalapa.

Elder Daniel Choc Xicay

LATTER-DAY SAINT MISSIONARIES IN THE 1976 GUATEMALA EARTHQUAKE

Elder Daniel Choc

Branch president Pablo Choc, his sons Elder Daniel Choc and Austin Choc, and Elder David Frischknecht behind the fallen church in Patzicía after most of the rubble was removed.

Read about Elder Choc's untimely death after the earthquake in 1976 on the pages Latter-day Saint Missionaries in the Guatemala Earthquake of 1976 and LDS Missionaries in the Guatemala Earthquake of 1976, Part 2.

On October 5, 2018, a "Noble And Great Ones" event was held in Salt Lake City to honor Latter-day Saint missionaries who lost their lives during their time of service. At that event, Larry Richman delivered a tribute to Elder Daniel Choc, the first full-time Latter-day Saint missionary from the town of Patzicía and the Church's first native Cakchiquel-speaking missionary.

Watch a video tribute to Daniel Choc by Larry Richman.

Below are the slides and text from the video tribute.

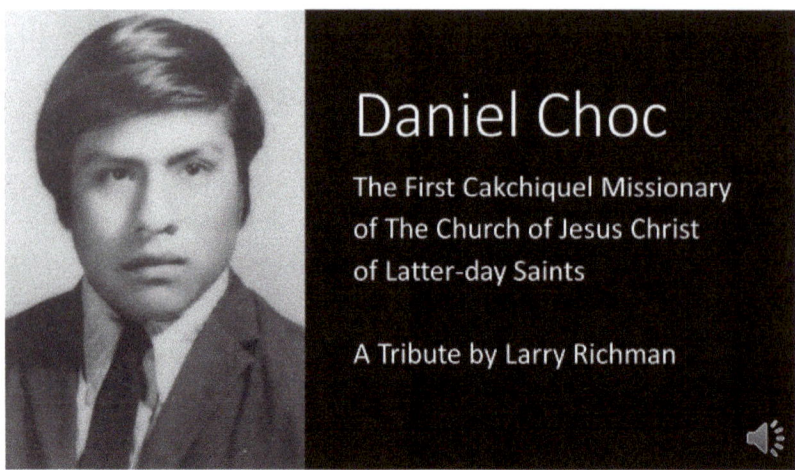

Daniel Choc was born December 11, 1952, in Patzicía, a little town of 5,000 people in the mountains of Guatemala.

This is a picture of Daniel and his family the day he left on his mission. He was the first missionary to serve from the town of Patzicía, in fact, from any of the Cakchiquel-speaking towns.

I was Elder Choc's missionary companion for 5 five weeks in the town of Comalapa. During those 5 weeks, he taught me things that I thought I already knew—like what dedication and commitment are all about. Elder Choc was an especially effective missionary—not only because he was a native speaker of Cakchiquel, but because he was humble, and had a way of explaining the gospel in a simple way that the Spirit could touch the hearts of the people. The most productive day of my entire mission was during those 5 weeks with Elder Choc. We taught 10 discussions that day. As we knocked on doors to find those 10 people to teach, and after being turned away at a door, Elder Choc would often run—not walk—to knock on the next door.

We had a somewhat unorthodox mission. In the Indian towns, all the men would go to work in the fields, and only women and children were at home during the day, so we would follow the men into the fields where we could teach them.

This is a picture of Elder Choc teaching a man and his son during a lunch break.

When the rains came, it didn't stop the work. The people still went to work in the fields, and so did we.

LATTER-DAY SAINT MISSIONARIES IN THE 1976 GUATEMALA EARTHQUAKE

On February 4, 1976, at 3:00am, an earthquake hit Guatemala. The quake measured 7.6 on the Richter scale and lasted 45 seconds. As you can see in this picture, adobe homes became rubble. The earthquake was 90 times stronger than the earthquake that leveled Managua, Nicaragua in 1972. That night, about 25,000 people died, 80,000 were injured, 250,000 homes were destroyed, and nearly 1.5 million people were left without shelter.

Even homes built of bricks came tumbling down.

This is the Church building in the town of Patzicía before the earthquake.

And after. Even the reinforced concrete beams weren't sufficient to withstand....

the force and shaking of the earthquake.

This is the inside of the cultural hall.

These are the remains of Daniel's family's home. The collapsed home killed his mother (who was pregnant at the time) and two of his brothers. Daniel's father was also the president of the Patzicía Branch. So not only did he have to deal with the death of his wife and three children, he was responsible for the members in the town who also had lost their homes.

In total, we buried 15 members who died in the town of Patzicía that night.

LATTER-DAY SAINT MISSIONARIES IN THE 1976 GUATEMALA EARTHQUAKE

Elder Choc soon returned from the town of Sumpango where he was serving at the time of the earthquake to comfort his father and his remaining family. This is a picture of his father, Pablo Choc on the left, then you see Elder Choc, his younger brother, and another missionary behind the fallen church in Patzicía after most of the rubble was removed.

In spite of the fact that Daniel had lost his mother and 3 siblings, he was on a mission. And he was undaunted in his commitment as a missionary. This is a picture taken days after the earthquake. Daniel (on the left) and another elder are teaching the nonmember husband of the Relief Society president who also died in the earthquake.

This is a picture of the baptism a few days later.

Elder Choc worked alongside the other missionaries for 2 months after the earthquake helping people shovel their way out of all the debris left by the devastating earthquake.

The few walls that remained standing were unsafe and had to be brought down. So we would pick away that the cement coating of the adobe or brick....

And then push the wall over.

Or pull it over. Two months after the earthquake, on March 29, 1976, we were working in the town of Patzún tearing down walls, when a wall similar to this gave way prematurely and fell. Everyone scrambled to safety, except for Elder Choc who was crushed by a four-foot section of brick and cement. A fellow missionary gave him artificial respiration while he was rushed to a nearby school that had been converted into a hospital.

But the Lord soon called him home. We thought we had seen the end of death from the earthquake two months before that, but now it took another life that was dear to us. All we could do was ask ourselves was "Why was it him under that wall and not me?" In spite of the difficulties he had in his life, Elder Choc was always happy and was a good friend to us. He was also an asset to the mission, being the only native Cakchiquel-speaking missionary. He patiently taught us to understand his people and to speak their language.

The mission president and I prepared Daniel's body and placed it in the casket. He was only about 5' 2", but he was a giant of a man in my eyes. We left on the lapel of his suit the button he wore which read "Por sacrificio se dan bendiciones" (Blessings come through sacrifice).

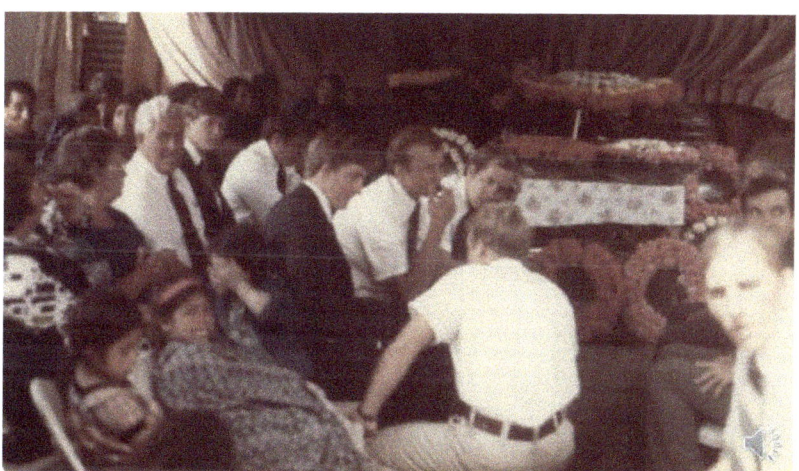

Missionaries and members at Elder Choc's funeral services.

Mission president Robert B. Arnold and Pablo Choc at the funeral. In his remarks, the mission president said, "I have had the privilege to interview Elder Choc and to know the intimate details of his life. I assure you that Elder Choc left this world completely dedicated and completely pure." "…I just hope I'm in as good a shape when I die as Elder Choc was."

I beheld that the faithful elders of this dispensation, when they depart from mortal life, continue their labors in the preaching of the gospel of repentance and redemption, through the sacrifice of the Only Begotten Son of God, among those who are in darkness and under the bondage of sin in the great world of the spirits of the dead.

D&C 138:57

Elder Choc was deserving of two honors. He was the world's first Cakchiquel missionary, and then he became the first Cakchiquel missionary in the spirit world. In D&C 138:57, we read of the vision given to President Joseph F. Smith about the spirit world: "I beheld that the faithful elders of this dispensation, when they depart from mortal life, continue their labors in the preaching of the gospel of repentance and redemption, through the sacrifice of the Only Begotten Son of God, among those who are in darkness and under the bondage of sin in the great world of the spirits of the dead."

Elder Choc's casket was placed in a tomb which was built over the grave of his mother, two brothers, and the twelve other members of the branch that we buried two months before that.

On the front of his tomb is a marble headstone with the following inscription: "When ye are in the service of your fellow beings ye are only in the service of your God. Mosiah 2:17. Daniel Choc (Xicay). Born December 11, 1953. Died March 29, 1976. The first Cakchiquel missionary of The Church of Jesus Christ of Latter-day Saints who died serving his people."

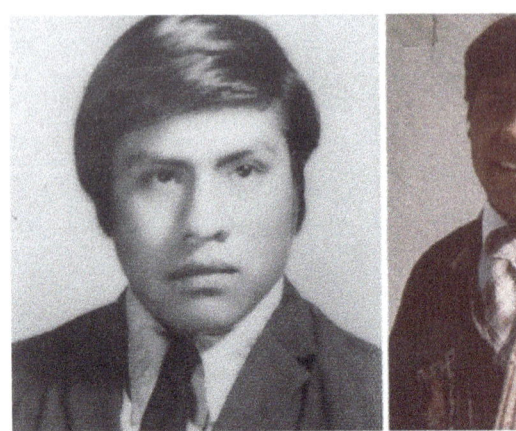

I love you, Elder Choc. I look forward to the day when I cross the veil and meet you again with open arms, and I can have the chance to thank you like I never really did in this life, for your friendship, and for the example you showed me.

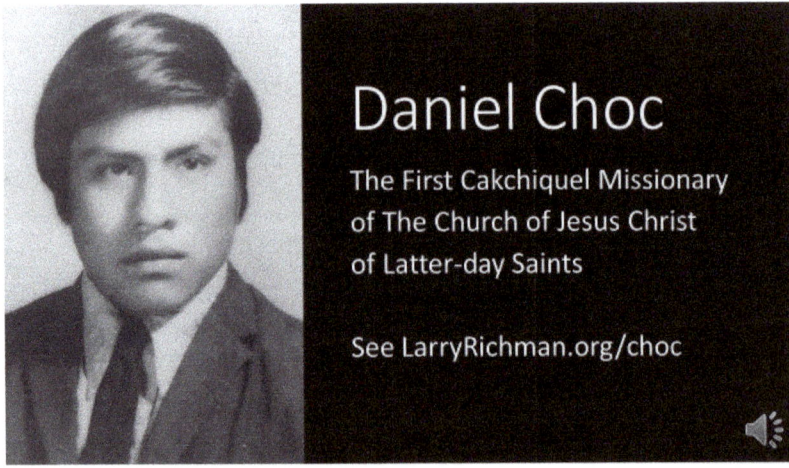

"I beheld that the faithful elders of this dispensation, when they depart from mortal life, continue their labors in the preaching of the gospel of repentance and redemption, through the sacrifice of the Only Begotten Son of God, among those who are in darkness and under the bondage of sin in the great world of the spirits of the dead." (Doctrine and Covenants 138:57)

www.ingramcontent.com/pod-product-compliance
Lightning Source LLC
Chambersburg PA
CBHW050030090426
42735CB00021B/3432